You can do it
FORGE FORWARD
EMPOWERING CHANGE
ISBN: 978-0-578-64381-6
ALL GOOD TODAY FOR THE BETTER
Keep going
Empower through
Gratitude is the way
ENJOY YOUR LIFE
Do what you love
I0339182

Wonder
positivity
I AM MAKING POSITIVE CHANGES!
optimism
Adventure
SATISFACTION

Hobbies
purpose
Love
INTEREST
INK
I AM DOING MY BEST!
Bliss
Passion

Love
play
I am enjoying life!
FUN
Entertainment
HAPPINESS

love
smile
AMUSE!
ENJOY
I am
optimistic
LAUGH!

I am grateful
FRIENDSHIP
BLESSING
FAMILY
Opportunities
idea
JOBS

Please your mind!
Play with interests!
Have fun
Love
Share love!
ENJOY MYSELF!
I AM ENCOURAGING POSITIVITY!

I live!
ACCOMPLISHED
I am a success!
I made it!
2 thrive
i SURVIVED!
I achieved!

I am loving!
I love choices
I love opportunities
I love friendships
I love fun
i LOVE ENTERTAINMENT

Amusing myself!
PLAYING WITH FRIENDS!
DOING WHAT I WANT
Entertaining myself!
Sharing what I love!
Love
I am enjoying!
Attending events!

Love
I am supporting good vibes!
I have awesomeness!
HAVE GOODNESS!
I HAVE LOVE!
I have a purpose!
I have blessings!

I AM WORTHY!
I MATTER!
I am amazing!
I AM COOL
I am wonderful!
I AM VALUABLE!
I MAKE A DIFFERENCE
I am awesome!

I am kind!
I do good!
I AM CARING!
I am respectful!
I give!
I am supportive!
fun
I HAVE A PURPOSE!
I SHARE!

I am worthy!
I PROVIDE VALUE!
I make a difference!
I AM AWESOME!
I do my best!
I am not a quitter!
I AM RESPONSIBLE!
I don't give up!

I love sharing my bliss
I AM MEANT TO SUCCEED!
I love having fun!
I AM THRIVING IN THE POSITIVITY!
I am awesome!
I LOVE SMILING AND SHARING!
I LOVE GOOD VIBES
I am meant to be happy

I AM LEARNING!
I am wiser
Learning from failing!
I know myself better!
I am growing!
I am stronger!
I AM SELF-IMPROVING!
I am smarter!

I AM PAVING MY WAY!
I am empowering through!
I am still loving my life!
I am staying positive!
I am forging forward!
I am still moving forward!
I AM MAKING THINGS HAPPEN
I am continuing on!

I ENJOY MAKING A DIFFERENCE
I AM WORTH THE TIME!
I have a good purpose!
I bring value to the world
I am amusing!
I am doing my best!
I am entertaining!
I do good things with my time!

I am supporting positive vibes!
I AM ATTRACTING GOOD PEOPLE!
I am supporting positive vibes!
I look forward to joy!
I CAN DO IT
I AM WONDERFUL
I enjoy celebrating!
I am manifesting good outcomes!

I AM WONDERFUL
TICKET
I AM A BLESSING IN THE FLESH!
ADMIT ONE
Ticket
I AM
AMAZING!
I am COOL!
THEATRE
I AM A SURVIVOR!
3D
I CAN DO IT!
I AM STRONG!
I am
BRAVE!

I bring value!
I Like ASSISTING
MATTER
I MAKE A POSITIVE DIFFERENCE!
I am worth it!
I am AWESOME
I am giving myself purpose!
I do good in the world!

I am giving my best!
I AM ENJOYING MY INTERESTS!
I am sharing my passion!
I am counting my blessings!
I AM MAKING THE BEST OF IT!
I am amusing myself
I AM RECEIVING WITH GRATITUDE!

I am succeeding!
I AM ENJOYING MYSELF!
honey
I AM PROGRESSING!
I am doing my best!
I am proud of myself
I AM BLISSFUL!
I AM SETTING GOALS!

I am respectful!
I AM GIVING THANKS!
I AM LOVING OTHERS!
LOVE
I AM APPRECIATIVE!
I AM FRIENDLY WITH OTHERS!
I am blessed!
I AM GRATEFUL!

I AM MAKING THE MOST OF MY LIFE!
I am going for my dreams!
I am not giving up!
I am making plans!
I am giving myself a purpose
AM ACCOMPLISHING MY GOALS!
I AM THRIVING ON THE GOOD!

I AM WORTHY ENOUGH!
I have what it takes!
I positively impact my life!
I bring value to others!
I am staying positive!
I am good!
I BELIEVE IN MYSELF!

I am looking forward to celebrating my milestones!
I am doing more with a positive attitude!
I AM PRACTICING OPTIMISM IN MY DAY!
I am looking forward to my success!
I AM LIVING WITH LOVE!
I am exercising gratitude with others!
I am looking ahead with enthusiasm!
I AM AMUSING MY THOUGHTS WITH GOODNESS!

I am manifesting good in my life!
I am creating my bliss within me!
I AM HAVING MORE FUN!
I AM ATTRACTING GOOD PEOPLE TO ME!
I AM ATTRACTING GOOD THINGS TO ME!
I am embracing joy!
I am living a blissful existence!
I am sharing my love with others!

I am bettering my interactions!
I am being more loving!
I AM DOING MORE GOOD FOR OTHERS!
am appreciating everything and everyone!
I am improving my relationships!
I am focusing on the positive!
I am bettering my life!
I AM PRACTICING MORE GRATITUDE!

I am bettering myself!
I am drinking healthier!
I AM NOT WASTING MY LIFE!
I AM COMMUNICATING BETTER!
I AM EATING HEALTHIER!
I AM THINKING MORE POSITIVE!
I am taking care of myself!
I AM THINKING BETTER!

I am creating my life!
I AM FORGING FORWARD!
I am empowering through
I am staying focused!
I am moving on!
I AM CONTINUING POSITIVELY!
I you
I am succeeding!
I AM SETTING GOALS!

www.ingramcontent.com/pod-product-compliance
Lightning Source LLC
Chambersburg PA
CBHW051150290426
44108CB00019B/2677
9780578643816